101 Amazing Animal Jokes for Kids

Joke Book for Kids

Ben Haydock

What do you call a bull while it sleeps?
- *A bull-dozer*

● ● ● ● ● ●

Why did the snake cross the road?
- *To get to the other ssside*

● ● ● ● ● ●

What did the buffalo say when to his son when he went to school?
- *Bison*

● ● ● ● ● ●

What do you call a fish with no eyes?
- *A fshhh*

● ● ● ● ● ●

How do bees go to school?
- *On the school buzz*

● ● ● ● ● ●

Why was the teddy bear not hungry?
- *Because he was stuffed*

● ● ● ● ● ●

Why is it easy to weigh a fish?
- *They have their own scales*

● ● ● ● ● ●

What happens when a cat eat a lemon?
- *They become a sour puss*

● ● ● ● ● ●

Why can't you play chess in the jungle?
- *There are too many cheetahs*

● ● ● ● ● ●

What is a crocodile's favorite game?
- *Snap!*

● ● ● ● ●

What happened to the frog's car when it broke down?
- *It was toad away*

● ● ● ● ● ●

What do you call a gorilla with his fingers in his ears?
- *Anything you want, he can't hear you*

● ● ● ● ● ●

What does a baby elephant take on holiday?
- *His swimming trunks*

● ● ● ● ●

What happened to the cat that swallowed a ball of wool?
- *She had mittens*

Where did the cow go on a date?
- *To the moo-vies*

What is black and white and red all over?
- *A penguin with a sunburn*

● ● ● ● ● ●

What do you call a bear without teeth?
- *A gummy bear*

● ● ● ● ● ●

Why do birds fly south for the winter?
- *Because it's too far to walk*

● ● ● ● ● ●

What do you get if you cross a centipede and a parrot?
- *A walkie-talkie*

● ● ● ● ● ●

What's a cat's favorite color?
- *Purrr-ple*

● ● ● ● ● ●

What does a cat eat for breakfast?
- *Mice Crispies*

● ● ● ● ● ●

What do you call a cow that has no legs?
- *Ground beef*

● ● ● ● ● ●

What do you call a cow when he's grumpy?
- *Moo-dy*

● ● ● ● ● ●

Knock Knock!
- Who's there?

Interrupting cow
- Interrupting cow wh…

Moo!

What do you call a dinosaur with no eyes?
- *Do you think he saw us?*

● ● ● ● ● ●

What does a dinosaur do when it sleeps?
- *It dino-snores*

● ● ● ● ● ●

What dog keeps the best time?
- *A watchdog*

• • • • • •

Why should you be careful when it rains cats and dogs?
- *Because you might step in a poodle*

• • • • • •

Why was the elephant poor?
- *Because he worked for peanuts*

● ● ● ● ● ●

What do you get when you cross a snowman and a shark?
- *Frostbite*

● ● ● ● ● ●

What fish only comes out when it's dark?
- *A starfish*

● ● ● ● ● ●

Where do fish sleep?
- *On the seabed*

● ● ● ● ● ●

What do frogs like to drink?
- *Croak-a-cola*

● ● ● ● ● ●

What do you call a horse living next door?
- *A neigh-bor*

● ● ● ● ● ●

How did the ape open the lock?
- *He used a mon-key*

● ● ● ● ● ●

Where does a gorilla hear gossip?
- *They hear it on the ape vine*

● ● ● ● ● ●

Where do hamsters live?
- *Hamsterdam*

● ● ● ● ● ●

Why did the spider buy a computer?
- *So he could surf the web*

● ● ● ● ● ●

What is orange and sounds like a parrot?
- *A carrot*

● ● ● ● ● ●

What did the penguin eat for lunch?
- *An iceberger*

● ● ● ● ●

What did the doctor give to the sick pig to make him better?
- *Oink-ment*

● ● ● ● ● ●

What kind of story do rabbits like?
- *Ones with a hoppy ending*

● ● ● ● ● ●

What is a snake's favorite subject at school?
- *Hiss-tory*

● ● ● ● ● ●

What key can't open a door?
- *A tur-key*

● ● ● ● ● ●

Why was the snail shy?
- *He wouldn't come out of his shell*

● ● ● ● ● ●

What did the fish say when he swam into a wall?
- *Dam!*

● ● ● ● ● ●

Why wouldn't the oyster share?
- *Because he was shellfish*

● ● ● ● ● ●

What is a toad's favorite music?
- *Hip hop*

● ● ● ● ● ●

Why don't penguins live in England?
- *They are afraid of Wales*

● ● ● ● ● ●

Why did the whale go to the concert?
- *To watch the Orca-stra*

● ● ● ● ● ●

What do you call a deer without any eyes?
- *No idea!*

● ● ● ● ● ●

What kind of snake tastes delicious?
- *A pie-thon*

● ● ● ● ● ●

What type of building does a sheep live in?
- *A baaarn*

● ● ● ● ● ●

What do cheetahs like to eat?
- *Fast food*

● ● ● ● ● ●

What did the cat say when his owner stepped on his tail?
- *Me-ow!*

● ● ● ● ● ●

What do you get when you cross a pig and a lumberjack?
- *A porkchop*

Where do fish keep their money?
- *In the river bank*

What do you call a kangaroo wearing a pullover?
- *A wooly jumper*

● ● ● ● ● ●

Why are mice afraid of water?
- *Because of the catfish*

● ● ● ● ● ●

How much does a male deer cost?
- *A buck*

● ● ● ● ● ●

What do alligators like to drink?
- *Gator-ade*

● ● ● ● ● ●

How did the duck pay for his meal?
- *He put it on his bill*

● ● ● ● ● ●

How do farmers count their cows?
- *They use a cow-culator*

● ● ● ● ● ●

Why can leopard's never play hide and seek?
- *Because they are always spotted*

What is the difference between a piano and a tuna?
- *You can tune a piano, but you can't tuna fish!*

● ● ● ● ● ●

What do you call a cat detective?
- *Purrlock Holmes*

● ● ● ● ● ●

What do you call a fly without wings?
- *A walk*

● ● ● ● ● ●

How did the prawn call his mother?
- *Using his shell-phone*

● ● ● ● ● ●

What did the pony say when his throat hurt?
- *I'm a little hoarse*

● ● ● ● ● ●

What is a bird's favorite subject at school?
- *Owl-gebra*

How does a penguin drink?
- *Out of a beak-er*

What do you call an Alligator that solves mysteries?
- *An investi-gator*

Where do sheep go to get their hair cut?
- *The baa-baa shop*

● ● ● ● ● ●

What type of shoes do frogs wear?
- *Open-toad sandals*

● ● ● ● ●

Why are barns always noisy?
- *Because all the cows had horns*

What do you call a rabbit with fleas?
- *Bugs bunny*

Why did the fish blush?
- *Because the seaweed*

● ● ● ● ● ●

What is a shark's favorite flavor sandwich?
- *Peanut butter and jellyfish*

● ● ● ● ●

Why do seagulls fly over the sea?
- *If they flew over the bay they would be called bagels*

Why do cows wear bells around their neck?
- *Because their horns don't work*

● ● ● ● ● ●

Why does a milking stool only have three legs?
- *Because the cow has the udder*

● ● ● ● ● ●

Why did the dog sit in the shade?
- *Because he was a hot dog*

● ● ● ● ● ●

What do you call a donkey with three legs?
- *A wonkey*

● ● ● ● ● ●

What do call a fish that's famous?
- *A starfish*

Why do fish like salt water?
- *Because pepper would make them sneeze*

Where do cows like to go on holiday?
- *Moo York*

● ● ● ● ● ●

What do you call a bear without any ears?
- *B*

● ● ● ● ● ●

Why did the cow cross the road?
- *To get to the udder side*

● ● ● ● ● ●

Which kind of dinosaur works for the police?
- *Tricera-cops*

● ● ● ● ● ●

Why do flamingos stand on one leg?
- *Because if they lifted the other one they would fall down*

● ● ● ● ● ●

How do dolphins make tough decisions?
- *They flipper coin*

● ● ● ● ● ●

What kind of music do cats like?
- *Purr-cussion*

● ● ● ● ● ●

What do you call a dog that likes baths?
- *A shampoodle*

● ● ● ● ● ●

What kind of guitar does a fish play?
- *Bass guitar*

● ● ● ● ● ●

Why are fish so clever?
- *They live in schools*

● ● ● ● ● ●

Where do baby cows eat lunch?
- *At the calf-eteria*

● ● ● ● ● ●

What do you call a bear that isn't smart?
- *A pan-duh*

● ● ● ● ● ●

Why can't an elephant use a computer?
- *Because they are afraid of the mice*

● ● ● ● ● ●

Why was the cat scared of the tree?
- *Because it was afraid of the bark*

● ● ● ● ● ●

What do you call a baby monkey?
- *Chimp off the old block*

● ● ● ● ● ●

What do you a very cold dog?
- *A pupsicle*

● ● ● ● ● ●

Thanks for reading *101 Amazing Animal Jokes for Kids*, now for you to go and test them out on your friends!

If you have enjoyed this book, please leave a *review* and check out our other titles.

Manufactured by Amazon.ca
Bolton, ON

39280871R00032